Roll the Dice

By Amanda Gebhardt

This game is fun!
Will you play it with Min?

This is a cube.
A cube has six sides.

 This is one side. It has dots.

These cubes are dice. Dice have these dots on each side.

 Min can roll these dice.

Min can add up dots.

This side is up.
It has five dots.

This side is up, too.
It has one dot.

Min can add them up. Six!

Min can move six spots.

Min is on this red space.

Now it is your turn!

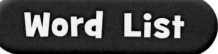

Word List

math words

cube
cubes
five
one
side
sides
six

sight words

a	play
A	roll
are	you
each	your
have	too
move	turn
one	

silent e

cube	five	sides
cubes	game	space
dice	side	these

Try It!

Roll a pair of dice. Add up the dots.

This game is fun! Will you play it with Min?

This is a cube. A cube has six sides.

This is one side. It has dots.

These cubes are dice.

Dice have these dots on each side.

Min can roll these dice. Min can add up dots.

This side is up. It has five dots.

This side is up, too. It has one dot.

Min can add them up. Six!

Min can move six spots.

Min is on this red space.

Now it is your turn!

Published in the United States of America by Cherry Lake Publishing Group
Ann Arbor, Michigan
www.cherrylakepublishing.com

Photo Credits: Cover: © Oleksii Kriachko/Dreamstime.com; pages 2, 6, 7, 11, 13: © Impact
Photography/Shutterstock.com; pages 3–5: © Gjermund/Shutterstock.com; pages 8–10, 15,
Back Cover: © dekede/Shutterstock.com; page 12: © Filip Fuxa/Dreamstime.com

Cherry Blossom Press is an imprint of Cherry Lake Publishing Group.

Library of Congress Cataloging-in-Publication Data has been filed and is available at catalog.loc.gov.

Cherry Lake Publishing Group would like to acknowledge the work of the Partnership for 21st Century
Learning, a Network of Battelle for Kids. Please visit http://www.battelleforkids.org/networks/p21
for more information.

Printed in the United States of America
Corporate Graphics

Amanda Gebhardt is a curriculum writer and editor and a life-long learner. She lives in Ann Arbor,
Michigan, with her husband, two kids, and one playful pup named Cookie.